D1433097

My First Picture Dictionary

Written by
Irene Yates

Illustrated by
Nick Sharratt

Consultant Editor Ginny Lapage

Collins
An imprint of HarperCollinsPublishers

Managing Editor: Jilly MacLeod
Art Director: Rachel Hamdi
Design Consultant: Sophie Stericker
Cover Designers: Susi Martin, Sonia Dobie
Designers: Holly Mann, Sarah Borny
Editor: Caroline Hind

First published in 2001 by HarperCollins*Children's Books*,
a division of HarperCollins*Publishers* Ltd
77-85 Fulham Palace Road, London W6 8JB

The HarperCollins website address is:
www.**fire**and**water**.com

On-line Support for Schools and Colleges
www.**Collins**Education.com

ISBN 0 00 198404 7

2 4 6 8 10 9 7 5 3 1

Printed in Hong Kong

Contents

How to use this book

It's never too early to share books with your child, to help them develop their language and literacy skills. This colourful dictionary has been designed with just that aim in mind. To get the most out of it, sit with your child and encourage them to talk about what they see, describing the pictures, naming the objects, and answering the questions.

First steps to reading

By coming back to the book time and again, your child will absorb many of the skills they will need when they start learning to read. They will expand their vocabulary, learn to look at words from left to right, and be able to recognize and match pictures, symbols, letters and words.

Tom

Elisha

Jake

Read the heading several times, running your finger along the line from left to right as you speak. Now allow your child to say the words, following the line with a finger.

Point to the headword and say it clearly, emphasizing the beginning sound.

Ask your child to name the object, and then to find it in the main picture.

Having fun at playschool

computer   teacher

book

scissors

Cats

paint   paintbrush

glue

crayons

12

Look for me on every page – sometimes you will have to look very hard! It's fun to see what I'm doing.

Lots of talking

The children introduced on these pages can be found throughout the book in a range of situations that will be familiar to your child. Help your child to recognize the characters by name, to talk about what each one is doing, and to enlarge upon what's happening on the page by telling you about their own experiences. Above all, encourage your child at all times to talk about what they see.

Help your child to answer the questions and follow any instructions. Make up your own questions as well, avoiding those that only require "yes" or "no" as an answer.

Encourage your child to tell you what each item is, then help them to "read" the word by running their finger along it from left to right, and saying it clearly.

Ask your child to match objects in the main picture with those shown on the left, and vice versa.

When looking for an object in the main picture, encourage your child to describe in words where it is – e.g. "It's on the table" – rather than simply pointing to it.

Encourage your child to tie the events in the picture to what's happening in their own life.

Lucy

Taz

Amy

Fun and games at home

door

window

chair

sofa

cushion

clock

television

telephone

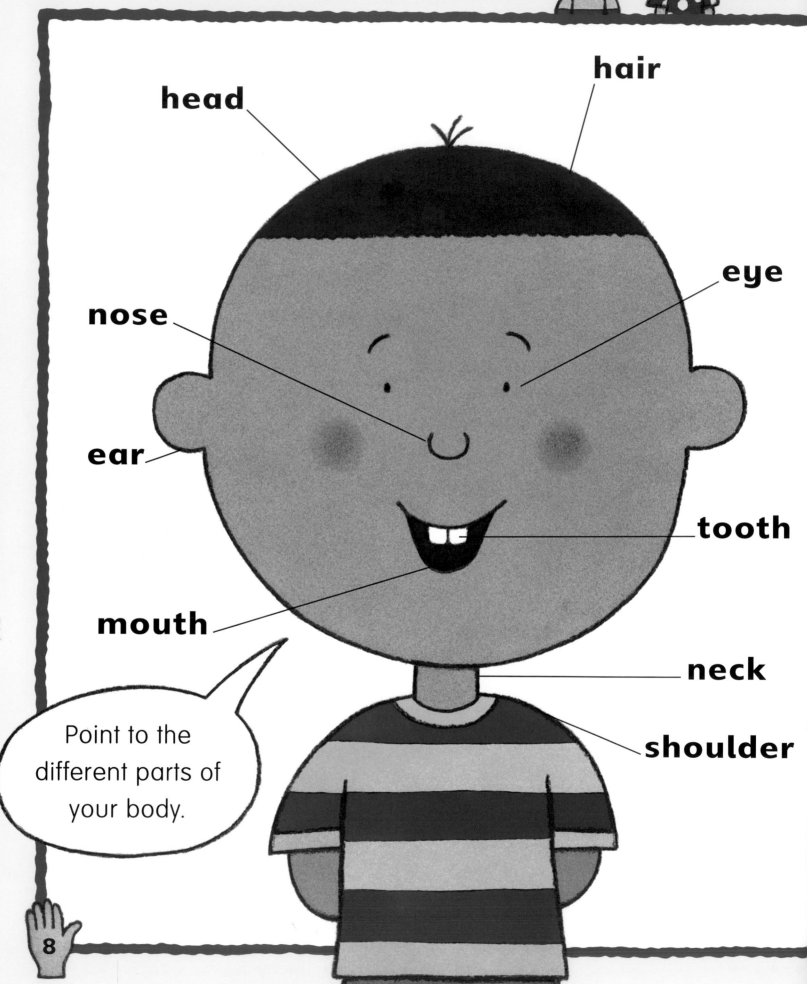

head

hair

eye

nose

ear

tooth

mouth

neck

shoulder

Point to the different parts of your body.

8

Come to my birthday party

balloon

mask

present

party hat

ice cream

cake

fruit juice

sweets

10

Having fun at playschool

computer

teacher

book

scissors

paint

paintbrush

glue

crayons

12

What do we like to wear?

jacket

shirt

dress

trousers

skirt

socks

shorts

Tell me about your favourite clothes.

shoes

14

What do you wear to go to bed?

pyjamas

nightie

pants

jumper

T-shirt

hat

gloves

15

Let's play in the garden

lawnmower

wheelbarrow

butterfly

bird

watering can

bike

paddling pool

flower

Take a walk down our street

house

car

street light

shop

wheelchair

policeman

traffic light

road

What colour means "stop"?

Things that go

rollerblades

lorry

motorbike

bus

digger

dumper truck

boat

skateboard

Let's go to the toy shop

jigsaw puzzle

truck

garage

doll's house

teddy bear

doll

puppet

blocks

22

At the supermarket

jar

bag

tin

basket

trolley

money

checkout

bottle

Food to help me grow

vegetables

fruit

rice

hamburger

chips

spaghetti

cereal

What do you eat for breakfast?

26

Take me to the pet shop

rabbit

hamster

kitten

puppy

goldfish

basket

cage

budgie

What's in the park?

slide

swing

buggy

climbing frame

bench

tree

dog

duck

30

Big beasts and minibeasts

kangaroo

giraffe

lion

elephant

panda

crocodile

whale

Down on the farm

farmer

tractor

hen

lamb

horse

cow

gate

hay

34

A sunny day at the seaside

shell

crab

seagull

sand castle

beach ball

wave

bucket

spade

See what we can do!

jump

walk

run

carry

clap

Which of these things do you like doing best?

paint

dance

38

What do you do when you feel sad?

sing

laugh

brush

cut

cry

eat

drink

39

Colours are everywhere

Come and count with me

1 one

How many windows does this house have?

2 two

3 three

4 four

5 five

42

Count the spots on the ladybird.

6 six

7 seven

8 eight

9 nine

10 ten

day

night

What do you do at night-time?

What is the weather like outside?

sun

rain

wind

snow

Index

47